European Colonies in the Americas

Dutch Colonies in the Americas

Lewis K. Parker

Rigby

Dutch Colonies in the Americas
Copyright © 2002 by Rosen Book Works, Inc.

On Deck™ Reading Libraries
Published by Rigby
a division of Reed Elsevier Inc.
1000 Hart Road
Barrington, IL 60010-2627
www.rigby.com

Book Design: Erica Clendening
Text: Lewis K. Parker
Photo Credits: Cover, pp. 4, 8, 9, 10–11, 12–13, 14–15, 18
© North Wind Picture Archives; p. 5 Erica Clendening; p. 7 © L. F.
Tantillo; pp. 16–17 © SuperStock; p. 17 © Stock Montage/SuperStock;
p. 19 © Hulton/Archive/Getty Images; p. 20 © Charles E. Rotkin/Corbis

On Deck™ is a trademark of Reed Elsevier Inc.

11 10 09 08
10 9 8 7 6 5 4 3 2

Printed in China

ISBN-10: 0-7578-2423-4
ISBN-13: 978-0-7578-2423-4

Contents

Henry Hudson

Early Dutch colonists came to America from a country called the Netherlands. In 1609, a Dutch trading company sent Henry Hudson to find a faster way to China and India.

Henry Hudson was an English sea captain. Hudson's ship was called the Half Moon.

The *Half Moon* on the Hudson River

4

Hudson did not find a faster way.
Instead, he found what came to
be called the Hudson River in
North America.

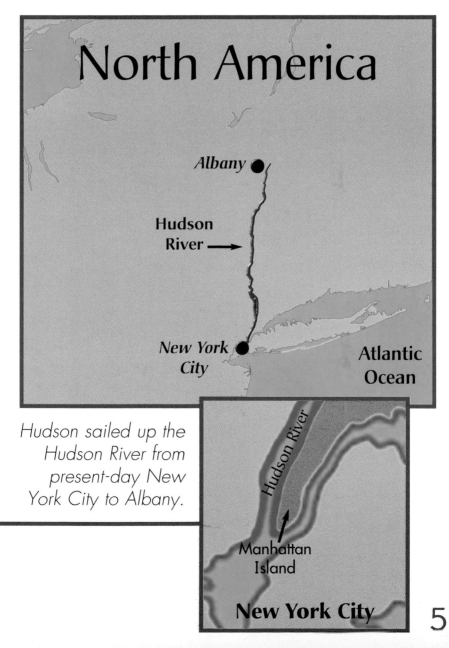

Hudson sailed up the
Hudson River from
present-day New
York City to Albany.

The Dutch West India Company

Soon, Dutch settlers came to the area that Hudson found. They called this area New Netherland. In 1621, the Dutch West India Company was formed in the Netherlands.

"The land is the finest for [farming] that I ever in my life set foot upon. . . . Never have I beheld such a rich and pleasant land."

—Henry Hudson's report to the Dutch government

The Dutch government gave the company control over New Netherland.

Dutch Settlements

In 1624, the company sent about 30 families to settle New Netherland. Some of the families set up the colony of New Amsterdam on the island of Manhattan.

Dutch settlers often traded for furs with Native Americans.

Other families settled in nearby places. The Dutch colonists traded for beaver and otter furs with the Native Americans living in the area.

In 1626, Peter Minuit (third from right) became the leader of New Netherland. He gave farm tools, glass beads, and cloth to the Native Americans for Manhattan Island.

The Dutch West India Company wanted to grow and make more money. To do this, the company needed more people in New Netherland. In 1628, the company started to give patroons, or rich people, large areas of land in New Netherland. In return, the patroons sent settlers to work on their land.

By the mid-1600s, New Amsterdam was a busy, growing city.

New Amsterdam was set up like towns in the Netherlands.

Many settlers cleared land to build farms in New Amsterdam. They cut down forests.

Dutch settlers and the Native Americans tried to live together in peace. However, they often fought against each other.

12

Native Americans living in the area became angry because they used the forests for hunting. This led to years of fighting.

New Amsterdam had other troubles, too. It became very dirty and unsafe. Buildings and streets were rundown. Garbage was thrown into the streets. There was a lot of fighting between the colonists.

Animals, such as pigs and cows, were allowed to walk through the streets in New Amsterdam.

The Fact Box

People from all over Europe came to live in New Amsterdam. About 20 languages were spoken in New Amsterdam.

Peter Stuyvesant

Peter Stuyvesant *(STUY-vuh-suhnt)* became
the leader of New Netherland in 1647.
Stuyvesant worked to make life in New
Amsterdam better. He fined people who
broke laws.

By 1664, *there were about 9,000
people living in New Netherland.*

He made people put up fences to keep animals off the streets. However, most people in the colony thought that Stuyvesant was too hard on them.

Before Stuyvesant came to New Netherland, he had been in charge of the Dutch colonies in the Caribbean Sea.

The End of New Netherland

In 1664, King Charles II of England gave his brother James, the Duke of York, land in North America. This land included New Netherland. James sent his navy to America to take control of the land. Stuyvesant wanted to fight the English.

The Dutch colonists did not want to go to war. They made Stuyvesant (raising his cane) give up control of the Dutch land to the English. This was the end of Dutch colonization in the Americas.

New Amsterdam was renamed New York, after James, the Duke of York.

Although the Dutch colonies in the Americas lasted only 40 years, they had a lasting effect on the people there. The Hudson River became an important waterway for moving people and goods.

New York City, today

New York City became a leading center for business. The Dutch colonies played an important part in American history.

Time Line

1609 Henry Hudson discovers the Hudson River.

1621 The Dutch West India Company is set up.

1624 Thirty Dutch families settle in New Netherland.

1625 New Amsterdam is founded.

1626 Peter Minuit becomes the leader of New Netherland. He buys Manhattan Island from the Native Americans.

1647 Peter Stuyvesant becomes the leader of New Netherland.

1664 The Dutch are forced to give up New Netherland to the English. New Amsterdam is renamed New York.

Glossary

Americas (uh-**mer**-uh-kuhz) the name used when speaking about North America, South America, and Central America

area (**air**-ee-uh) a part of certain place

Caribbean Sea (kar-uh-**bee**-uhn **see**) a sea that borders the West Indies, Central America, and South America

colonists (**kahl**-uh-nihsts) people who come to live in colonies

colonization (kahl-uh-nuh-**zay**-shun) when colonies are set up

colony (**kahl**-uh-nee) a faraway land that belongs to or is under the control of a nation

effect (uh-**fehkt**) the result of something

patroons (puh-**troonz**) people who own large areas of land

settlers (**seht**-luhrz) people who come to stay in a new country or place

Resources

Books

Peter Stuyvesant: Dutch Military Leader
by Joan Banks and Arthur M. Schlesinger
(Senior Consulting Editor)
Chelsea House Publishers (2000)

The New York Colony
by Dennis Brindell Fradin
Children's Press (1988)

Web Site

Get the Facts About New York State
http://www.dos.state.ny.us/kidsroom/
    nysfacts/factmenu.html

Index

C
colonists, 4, 9, 14, 18
colony, 8, 17, 20–21

D
Duke of York, 18–19
Dutch West India
    Company, 6, 21

H
Hudson, Henry,
    4–6, 21
Hudson River, 5,
    20–21

N
Native Americans,
    8–9, 12–13, 21
New Amsterdam,
    8, 10–12, 14–16,
    19, 21
New Netherland,
    6–10, 16–18, 21

P
patroons, 10

S
settlers, 6, 8, 10, 12
Stuyvesant, Peter,
    16–18, 21